The Eleven Touches to a Happy Marriage

Gordon Greenhalgh, Ph.D.

Eleven Touches to a Happy Marriage

Gordon Greenhalgh, Ph.D.

Askdrgordon.com

Published by Family Care Publications

ISBN: 9781494299743

Dedication

To my wife Cheri, who has inspired me and taught me
much of what is in this book

Contents

Introduction

The goal of this book is to provide you with the tools to improve your marriage and to help both of you create the kind of marriage that will bring happiness instead of strife, conflict and disappointment.

Most of us don't have the time, money, or inclination to spend on counseling, workshops, or reading books to improve our marriage. But face it most marriages could use a little help.

Having practiced as a licensed marriage and family therapist for over 25 years, I developed some simple and quick strategies to improve your marriage. If you read this book and implement my exercises you will find significant improvement in your marriage, without the cost and time of therapy or workshops.

Marriage is like a garden that needs to be tended on a regular basis. If not, it starts to die. Weeds and bugs will slowly devour the untended garden. So many marriages fail because men and women are not being tended to in a way that meets their needs. As a result, there comes conflict, distance, lack of intimacy, and acting out in destructive ways.

Men need to feel respected and desired. Women need to feel safe and loved. Learn to do that for your spouse. Then you'll find that they will be able to give back what you need. This book will show you the most important things to focus on in order to meet your mate's needs. Having done that, you will find yourself experiencing a happy marriage.

Chapter 1

The Understanding Touch

Men and women are so different that they truly do not understand each other. It is one of the biggest problems I see in marriage counseling. It is as if we are two different species. To make progress in our marriages, we must expand our understanding of our spouses.

When we feel understood, it opens our hearts and minds to the person who touches us in that way. Giving this understanding touch is the foundation to building your marriage. So how do you do it? Here are some helpful hints:

Listen!

Shut up! Turn the T.V. off. Put the newspaper down and really listen. You can't possibly understand someone if you don't take the time to listen.

It makes us feel special if someone takes the time to give us their undivided attention. People pay me $120.00 an hour to get it. You don't have to understand all the nuances of the opposite sex in order to listen. Nor does it take a Ph. D. to respond in a way that shows you are listening and understand what you are hearing. It is probably one of those things you did well when you were courting.

Listening means you care. Listening means you love. If you don't take the time to listen, your spouse will feel that you don't really care very much about them. You can say that you love and care, but you have to *show* it in order for it to work. Working on it for just 15-30 minutes a day can make a big difference in your relationship.

It will also be important to set it up right. Don't be distracted, too tired, too hungry, or not in a good mood. Find a time and find a way. It's important!

Show Empathy

To empathize with someone is to have the ability to put yourself in their shoes and feel what they feel. If you can try to be them and see it from their perspective, it will help you understand your spouse. It doesn't mean that you have to agree with them, but that you can at least see where they may be coming from.

Once you can do that, then you can respond by saying such things as...

-It sounds like you are feeling...

-I can see why you feel...

-I would feel that way too if...

This ability to show empathy is crucial to giving the understanding touch that will calm and open the heart of your spouse.

A note to men here: We tend to problem solve. We want to fix it. Women just want to know that you *understand* and *care* about how they feel. If you do that, I promise you it will work much better than coming up with a solution.

Validate

Generally, if you don't validate someone's feeling or position, they don't feel understood. We may be so busy and intent on getting our own point across that we fail to validate the other person and their perception of reality.

As a therapist, I often mediate problems between people. I have learned that before I can put in my two cents worth, I must first validate each person's position. Once again, it doesn't mean I must agree. I just need to show an understanding and a sense of value to each person. How can I do that when I totally disagree with them, or if I think they are being selfish or ridiculous?

The answer is to look for something you can

validate. First listen, then show empathy, then either validate the person ("I can see you have good intentions..." or "I know you are an intelligent person") or validate their feelings ("I can understand how you feel" or "I'm sorry you feel..."). You can also validate their position ("I can see why it makes sense to do that..." or "You're right about that, but...").

Find some aspect of the situation to validate before expressing your own feelings, position, or needs. Your spouse will feel most understood when you are able to validate them. And this can decrease the amount of turmoil and conflict you're experiencing.

The understanding touch is crucial to improving your marriage. Knowing how and why men and women are different will increase your understanding. The more you educate yourself in this area, the better your relationship can be. Just listen, show empathy, and validate. You will be amazed at how things will change as you implement these strategies.

Chapter 2

The Hurting Touch

Before we address the remaining positive touches, we need to take a look at the touch that will undermine the goal of improving your marriage. To be successful, you must stop or greatly minimize the hurting touch. Your relationship will not work well if you operate with a hurting touch on a regular basis. Even though you may be fairly successful with the other eleven touches, a hurting touch will sabotage your efforts.

I have identified ten hurting touches, and developed an Assessment Questionnaire to see how you are doing in these areas. It is important to be honest with yourself. I would suggest that you and your spouse grade each other to see if you are in agreement.

Assessment Questionnaire

Grade yourself on each statement according to the following scale:

(3) Almost always true.
(2) Sometimes true.
(1) Rarely true.
(0) Never true.

A. Selfish

_____ It is rarely my fault when something goes wrong in the family or when we argue.

_____ I'm too busy to give much time to my spouse and

family.

_____ I expect to be served instead of serving.

_____ I seldom sacrifice my wants and needs for someone else's.

_____ I often resent the time my kids require of me, and often don't give up my time.

B. Inconsistent

_____ My spouse rarely knows how I will react in any given situation. I may be loving and kind one minute, then harsh or abusive the next.

_____ I don't let my spouse know my plans. He/she is never sure when I'll be home or where I am.

_____ I don't always do what I say I'm going to do.

_____ My discipline of the kids is inconsistent and sporadic.

_____ My mood is rarely consistent. My family has to walk on eggshells around me.

C. Irresponsible

_____ I have trouble maintaining a steady job and income.

_____ I don't take care of household responsibilities in a timely manner, or I must be nagged to get things done.

_____ I often spend money unwisely.

_____ I often forget appointments.

_____ I rarely take care of the kids.

D. Passive

_____ I'm rarely in charge of anything.

_____ I keep my anger in, or allow it to build up and explode after a time.

_____ My spouse makes most of the decisions.

_____ I have trouble disciplining the kids.

_____ I'm easily influenced by my friends, or have no friends.

E. Abusive

_____ I verbally attack my spouse or kids with yelling, profanity, or cruel insulting words.

_____ I physically attack my family by hitting, shoving, or slapping.

_____ I force my spouse to have sex with me even if he/she doesn't want to.

_____ I degrade my family through intimidation, threats (money, physical abuse), or by instilling fear.

_____ My spouse and kids are fearful of me.

F. Insensitive

_____ I rarely give my spouse my undivided attention.

_____ I pay little attention when someone is hurting or upset.

_____ I'm not sure how to meet the emotional needs of my spouse.

_____ I'm accused of not caring.

_____ I spend little time listening to my children.

G. Lazy

_____ My spouse often nags me about doing things around the house.

_____ I spend a lot of time in front of the T.V.

_____ My spouse takes care of the kids.

_____ I do few physical, mental, or spiritual exercises.

_____ It's easier to stay home.

H. Overbearing

_____ I am seldom wrong and I let my family know it.

_____ I don't really consider or respect my spouse's opinion, feelings, and ideas.

_____ I see everything as black or white, right or wrong.

_____ I seldom give my kids my complete attention when they talk, and when I do, it's to show them that they're wrong.

_____ I seldom compromise.

I. Inconsiderate

_____I sometimes forget special days such as birthdays or anniversaries.

_____ I seldom go out of my way to do extra special things on those special days.

_____ I don't think about what my children need. Instead I think about what I want them to do.

_____ I usually treat others more considerately than I treat my spouse and family.

_____ I conveniently forget many requests my spouse asks of me.

J. Disrespectful

_____ I sometimes put my spouse down in front of others.

_____ I really don't value my spouse's input in a situation.

_____ I treat my kids as though they were inferior.

_____ I use words like stupid, imbecile, idiot, or worse

when talking to my spouse or kids.

_____ I'm generally disrespectful to those in authority.

Now add up all your points. The following will indicate where you stand.

Scores

0-35: A spouse whose non-loving behavior is minimal and who is probably not experiencing great distress in the marriage.
36-70: A spouse whose non-loving behavior is causing some problems and who needs to work on some changes.
71-150: A spouse whose non-loving behavior is significant, and who is probably having great distress in the marriage. He/she needs to take some immediate action to change the situation.

Hopefully you did fairly well on the test. All of us have some undesirable qualities that need improving. However, if you did poorly, the chances of having a satisfied spouse and family are slim until changes are made.
After getting your score, go over each category and rank them from best to worst. In which categories did you score the best? These are your strengths. In which categories did you have the most problems? These are where you need to focus your energy on changing.
I assume you love your spouse and children. You wouldn't be reading this if you didn't. It's likely that you need and want to improve in this area. The hurting touch will destroy your relationship. No one is perfect. We all fail at times. But if you are consistently hurting your family, I recommend that you get some professional help.

Most marriages fail because there is a lack of positive touches, and a presence of hurting touches. The goal of this book is to identify and increase the positive touches. But we must also work diligently to address and eliminate the hurting touches.

Chapter 3

The Healing Touch

Let's face it. Life is tough. We all get hurt. Not only do we all get hurt, we all cause hurt. The reason so many marriages fail is because of the damage that has been done. Our hurt and pain quickly turn into anger and bitterness that erodes the foundation of our love. Eventually we lose our positive feelings and we lose our connection. Then we lose our commitment.

Unfortunately, it is not possible to be in a close relationship and not hurt the person you're with. We are all imperfect people who lack in the ability to give and show love 100% of the time. We want to improve on our ability to love, but even so we will fail at times, and hurt the one we love. When that happens, we need to find a way to bring about healing. Then our relationship can move forward instead of regressing and crumbling. We need a healing touch.

A healing touch requires a sufficient apology from the offending spouse. It also requires forgiveness from the hurt spouse. Without these two ingredients, you will not achieve healing. You will continue to have a wall of hurt, pain, anger, and bitterness standing between you and your spouse. That will interfere with the love that both of you want to experience. Let's take a look at the ingredients of healing necessary to create the relationship you truly desire.

Sufficient Apology

It isn't as simple as just saying "I'm sorry." A sufficient apology has the necessary elements to allow the hurt person to feel understood, accepted, and loved. That makes it easier for them to forgive, bringing about healing and reconciliation.

In Gary Chapman's and Jennifer Thomas' book, *The Five Love Languages of Apology,* they break down these important elements of apology based on their own extensive research. Let me briefly share the five fundamental aspects or "languages" of an apology that they have discovered.

1) Expressing Regret

The best way to express regret is to look your spouse in the eye and say, "I'm sorry," you need to be sincere and genuine. It needs to be said in a soft, loving manner, not in harshness or anger. You want to communicate that you are truly regretful for your actions.

2) Accepting Responsibility

Accepting responsibility is admitting that you were wrong. Our tendency is to blame someone else for our mistakes or inappropriate behavior. We want to excuse, justify, rationalize, or minimize our wrong doing. To say "I'm sorry," followed by "but..." is not accepting responsibility for your actions. When you accept responsibility, then your apology will more likely be accepted.

3) Making Restitution

If your attitude in the apology is one of having a desire to correct the wrong and figure out what you can do to make it right, thereby providing some form of restitution, you are making good strides toward healing and restoration.

Our natural human tendencies cause us to cry out for justice. Justice often demands more than saying, "I'm sorry," and accepting responsibility. We must attempt to do something that will make things right, and create a feeling of justice. When that happens, then restoration of the relationship is much more likely.

4) Genuinely Repenting

Gary Chapman states: *"Repentance is more than saying, 'I'm sorry; I was wrong. How can I make it up to you?' It is also saying, 'I'll try not to do this again.' For some individuals, it is repentance that convinces them that the apology is sincere. The offending person's repentance, then, elicits the offended person's forgiveness."*

To repent means to turn around, to go in the opposite direction. To repeatedly hurt your partner over and over in the same way will not bring about forgiveness. Therefore, it is likely that real change needs to happen. It will be important to develop a plan of change in order to create change. You can't expect healing and forgiveness without implementing some real change in your life. Develop your plan and implement it.

5) Requesting Forgiveness

To actually go to your spouse and say, "will you forgive me?" may be more difficult than you think. Dr. Chapman states that, *"many people will fear losing control, fear being rejected, or fear failure."* These issues make requesting forgiveness difficult. However, for some people requesting forgiveness sends a positive message of regret and of accepting responsibility along with a desire for restoration. It is yet another language of apology.

Hopefully, these different apology languages that I outlined from Dr. Chapman will be helpful in breaking down the barriers of forgiveness and the walls of anger and hurt that interfere with intimacy.

For a couple to have a happy marriage it is necessary to experience healing when we have been hurt. Without the healing there will always be the walls of protection that block true connection and intimacy.

Chapter 4

The Caring Touch

You care about and for your spouse. Even couples who are having significant problems can still give a caring touch. We need to be taken care of and we need someone to deeply care for us.

What then is the best way to give that caring touch? It is not enough to say you care. It *must* be shown. You can care to the nth degree, but it will not do much good for you or your spouse if you are unable to demonstrate that caring in ways that really work.

Men and women generally need different caring touches. To be effective, you will need to understand and give the caring touch your spouse so desires. I will give you four caring touches for both men and women. In general, I think you'll find these gender differences accurate. Check it out with your spouse to make sure you're on the right track.

MEN:

1. Care about my job.

A man's job is one of the most important areas of his life. Many times his job is the top of the list. If you don't care about his job, then he will think you don't care much about him. His job is what he spends most of his time on, what he thinks and worries about most. Men feel pressure to provide for their families. Even if the wife works outside the home, the man is typically the one who feels the pressure of providing. A man who doesn't do well in this area often feels inadequate as a man, and he struggles with self-esteem problems.

Show you care by asking him about his day, the problems, the pressures, the failures, the fears, the hopes. Listen and show empathy, like you do with your girlfriends. Men often don't want advice about their work. If they do, they will ask. Giving unsolicited advice triggers feelings of inadequacy and won't go over very well. Show that you understand and care about the financial pressure he is dealing with.

2. Care about my physical needs.

Men are like little boys. We want to be taken care of. Feed us, have sex with us, let us play, take care of the home. There is nothing wrong with these needs and desires. If you care about them and attend to them, your man is more likely to feel satisfied but and in addition have good feelings about you.

Granted there are too many men who never grow up and expect their wives to mother them way too much. Of course, men need to balance out being taken care of, with taking care of his wife and children. The key is to find that balance. Giving too much or giving too little in this area will inevitably lead to problems.

3. Show you care by appreciating me.

It may seem a bit childish, but men need appreciation. They respond well when they feel appreciated. Many wives will say "Why do I have to thank him or show appreciation for helping me with the children, or helping me around the house. It's his house and children too!" Why? Because it is a caring touch that your man needs, and it will reap benefits for you directly. When a man feels appreciated, then he is more motivated to help and please you. If a man feels unappreciated, or even worse, feels that his efforts are inadequate, he will likely not continue. If you want your husband to do certain things, then show appreciation for what he does. It really isn't that hard. All it takes is a touch or hug with a few positive words.

4. Show you care by respecting me.

Men need respect more than they need sex. If you don't believe me, then ask a man if he would rather live with a woman who respects him, or a woman who only wants sex with him.

Respect is crucial for a man in a relationship. Without respect, there will be significant problems. You may be wondering how you can respect him when he has acted in some very disrespectful ways. Good question. I'm not saying you should respect destructive, inappropriate, or non-loving behavior. Focus on respecting who he is. The fact that you are with him says you found some positive things that you respect about him. Obviously he cannot be all that you want. Let's face it-he is a man. However, you can still respect his desires, his motivation, his attempts to please you, to meet your needs, and his attempts at trying to love you.

If you are constantly critical, emasculating, negative, complaining, instructing, belittling him, then you are not being respectful.

It is possible to show respect to anybody regardless of what they have done. It doesn't mean you don't address unhealthy behavior. It means you show respect in the process.

WOMEN:

1. Care about my feelings.

Most men are uncomfortable when it comes to

feelings. We don't like to feel too much. We aren't good at expressing feelings or hearing someone express feelings to us. We are not quite sure what to do about it. Feelings scare us and trigger our own feelings of insecurity.

Well, too bad. Quit being an emotional wimp. Your wife needs to express her feelings. She needs to talk things out, and she needs you to express your own feelings. So get tough. Prepare yourself to listen and empathize. It is not as hard as you think. Most men go into the problem solving mode, but women don't want solutions. They want you to listen and try to understand what they're feeling and why. Put yourself in their shoes – that is empathy. It will work and it shows you really care about your spouse.

2. Give me non-sexual attention.

Women already know you want and like their bodies. What they really need to know is that you want and like who they are. If you are always focused on sex and her sexual parts, then she won't feel that you really care for her. Start giving non-sexual affection daily. Hold her hand, give her a warm hug (without grabbing her butt), cuddle, soft kisses, massages, brush her hair. All go a long way in showing you really care about her.

Be romantic without being sexual. Giving cards, flowers, romantic dinners, dancing, and love notes really give a touch of caring without focusing on sex. If you can focus on giving non-sexual attention then my guess is it will lead to more sex. But let her take you there. You need to focus on giving affection as an end in itself.

3. Treat the children in caring ways.

One of the best ways to show how much you care about your wife is to demonstrate caring behavior to the kids. Nothing is closer to a woman's heart than her children. When she sees you loving them in tender, positive ways, she will feel very cared for by you and will be drawn to you.

Now I know you care for your kids, but the important thing here is how well you show that you care. There are specific ways to operate with kids that will be most effective. Consider the following:

A) Spend time doing fun things with your kids, things that they want to do.

B) Be involved in their activities, school, and friends. Be interested in their lives.

C) Don't be harsh with your words or behavior toward them. Respect your children even if you don't like their behavior.

D) Communicate your love and commitment to your kids even in the light of discipline.

E) Discipline your children in constructive ways. If you don't know how, then learn.

We'll touch a little more on this subject in Chapter Six. The point here is caring for your children is one of the best ways to give your wife a caring touch.

4. Show you care by protecting me.

One of a woman's primary needs is to feel safe and secure. She needs you to help provide her with that security. It will show her how much you care. There are three ways to give her that protective touch: financial, physical, and emotional.

To protect her financially is to do your best to be a good provider by working hard to make money as well as learning how to manage it.

To protect her physically is to take into account her fears about safety for her and the children. Respect her need to lock doors, to have an alarm system, and being careful with the kids. If it makes her feel safer, then do it, even if it doesn't make sense to you. It is a great way to show you care. Above all, don't you be the one who hurts her. If you can't control your anger and you hurt your wife, then please get some help. It's not her fault if you lose your temper and do damage. That is your choice and your problem.

Protecting your wife emotionally is learning to understand and attend to her feelings as I stated earlier. She needs to feel safe with you emotionally in order to move toward you and feel that you really care.

The result of taking the time and effort to give the caring touch to your spouse will bring many rewards. Though learning to adequately give this touch will take some effort, it will be worth it.

Chapter 5

The Helping Touch

We all need help. There is too much to do, we all have too much on our plates. That is the nature of life. It is why one of the biggest complaints I hear in counseling with couples is "I need more help, can't you help me around here more?" When someone is feeling "put upon", or feels like they are carrying most of the burden, they will start building resentment, undermining the good feelings and satisfaction in a marriage.

It is often difficult to overcome this issue because there is always too much to do and never enough time. However, if a couple doesn't come to some resolution in this area, it will be an ongoing barrier to accomplishing their goals of a good relationship.

Let me provide some basic principles that may help you provide the helping touch.

1. Work is work.

The first principle to understand is there's no such thing as women's work or men's work. Work is just work. It needs to be done. Both of you need to be willing to do the work. How many times have I heard "That's a woman's job or that's a man's job?" No, it's not – it is just work.

Now that we have established that, it will be important to gravitate toward the kind of work that you are best at, as it will be what you are more inclined to do. Most couples will normally end up doing this. I often find women who want to work in the yard and men who like to do the cooking. It doesn't really matter. What matters is that the two of you learn what is going to work best, and that the work is evenly distributed, which leads to the second principle.

2. Communicate, compromise, and implement your work plan.

Resolving this issue will require communicating, compromising, and implementing. The first step is to make a list of the work that needs to be done. Unfortunately, it will probably be a long list. Once the list is completed, then go over each item one at a time. As you go over the list, volunteer to take on jobs that are most suited to your abilities and interest. Skip the ones that neither of you want or both of you want. First take care of the jobs you both agree on.

The second step is where compromise comes in. If you want your relationship to work, you are going to have to do things you don't want to do. Let's face it. Sorry, that's life, so now go over the rest of the list and figure who is going to do what. Keep in mind that you love your spouse and you should want to try and help them. Keep in mind you may have the option to hire out some of the work or, heaven forbid, get your kids to help. Keep communicating and compromising until you have delegated all the work that needs to be done.

Now it is just a matter of implementing what you have both agreed upon. Which leads to the next principle...

3. Women stop nagging – Men start doing.

Many relationships end up with women mothering their men in order to get things done. Women will nag, complain, criticize, and try to control men. As you have probably found out, it doesn't work so well. So I have an idea – stop it. Don't focus on trying to get him do anything. Men just don't respond well to that. I'm sure you're wondering then, "What am I going to do?" Okay,

I'll give you a few suggestions. First, it's okay to tell him what you want or how you feel:

"I feel hurt or taken advantage of when you don't help me."

"I would really appreciate it if you could do this for me."

"Can you help me here? I would be so grateful."

"It angers me when you ignore what I need."

So tell him, just don't repeat it over and over, and don't try to force or manipulate to get what you want. Instead decide what *you* are going to do if something doesn't happen:

"It would really make me feel better if this were done. If you can't take care of it for me, then I'll hire someone to take care of it."

"Is there some reason that you haven't been able to do that? Is there something I can do to make it happen?"

"I am so upset about this that I need to get away for a while."

"I plan to set up a counseling appointment to help me deal with this problem; I am hoping that you will come with me."

Don't try to change someone else. Decide on what would be the most constructive action, and then do it.

Men, if you don't want to be mothered, controlled, or nagged, then quit acting like a teenager. Man up and do the responsible things. Your wife shouldn't have to tell you to do anything. You're an adult, a grown man, so take action and take care of business. Let your wife know what you plan to do, how you plan to do it, and when it will be done. Then make sure you do it. You will increase the chances of your wife getting off your back, and letting you take care of it. Remember, ladies, your way is not the only way. If you criticize your spouse for doing things differently than you, it's likely he will just stop doing it.

If you will both sit down and do the work list, decide who is doing what and when, then you'll be able to avoid much of the conflict and problems. Then you can rest and enjoy each other, which leads to the final principle.

4. We need rest and recreation.

Recreation and having fun is crucial to a healthy relationship. Most couples I see in therapy are sorely lacking in having fun together. It is what brought you together in the first place, and then because of "life" we stop having fun. It is usually one of the first homework assignments I give to couples. Spend 2-3 hours per week just having fun with each other. Take the time, schedule it and do it.

Chapter 6

The Kid's Touch

One of the most common areas of conflict in marriages revolves around issues with the kids. Raising children is one of the toughest jobs on earth, with both great rewards and great heartaches. There is nothing that we have more of an emotional investment in than our kids. With such a great emotional investment, we are more likely to react quickly and strongly, often leading to anger, hurt, anxiety, and conflict.

My goal in this chapter is to give you a few tools that can improve the kid's touch, leading to a more harmonious marriage. Obviously, one short chapter on parenting cannot begin to cover the multitude of strategies, issues, and problems that arise in being a parent. If you are having significant problems in this area, I would suggest going to the bookstore, or counseling center, or parent workshop to improve your skills. Good parenting is learned. It is not automatic or instinctual.

The following steps will give you a good foundation to create a positive parenting experience.

The first tool is *unity.* Parents need to be unified in their approach to handling the kids. One of the best parenting strategies is a healthy marriage. So many couples are not working together but in opposition to each other, which leads to undermining any effective parenting. When kids see their parents working together, then it gives them a firm foundation of love and stability. Whatever parenting techniques are employed will then be that much more effective.

What I find in most families is the tendency toward extremes. One parent is too harsh, the other too lenient. One is over parenting, the other is under parenting. One is too strict, the other too permissive. One is too demanding, while the other one expects too little. One is over involved, the other is under involved. You get the picture.

This is why parents fight and don't work as a team. If parents work together they will create balance, and provide the optimum parenting environment. So, how do you do this? You have a business meeting. The business at hand is parenting your child. First, you establish the time and place for the meeting. Second, listen to each other about the problems or issues. Third, make recommendations to improve the situation. Fourth, validate each other's observations and suggestions. Fifth, determine the best course of action. Sixth, decide how to implement the action, and seventh, implement the action. These seven steps can create an atmosphere of communication, compromise, change, and unity.

Love is the second tool of effective parenting. You have to love your kids. I know you have already figured this one out, but let me expound on it some. I know you love your kids. The key is knowing how to communicate that love so they really feel loved, valued and cherished.

How do you then communicate this to a child? No matter the age, it boils down to primarily three things: time, attention, and respect.

Time: Your child needs you to spend focused time on them. Play with them, have fun, do what they want (within limits). Parents are so busy taking care of life that they fail to have enough positive, connecting time with their children. One on one time is best. They need it from both parents on a very regular basis. Focus on them and have fun.

Attention: Look at me! Look at me! How many times have you heard your young children say these words? I've got news for you. It never goes away. You can be 50 years old and you still need you parents to look at you. Pay attention to me. Show me that I am valuable and that you really care.

This is translated in attending their events, activities, and school functions. Be involved in their lives. Be interested in their friends, fears, opinions, and experiences. Pay attention to them.

Respect: This is what I find most lacking in parents. This leads to children, especially teenagers, who then don't respect their parents. You may think that just because you're the parent you should be respected, but it doesn't work that way. When kids feel respected then they generally give it, when they don't feel respected, they definitely won't give it.

We yell, we don't listen, we ignore, we mistreat, we don't validate, and we are downright mean to our kids. Then we wonder why we have angry, disrespectful teenagers. You can always treat your kids with respect, no matter what their behavior is. Sure, it may be difficult, but you are able to treat them with respect even if you don't like them or want to. Take for example the annoying neighbor, the cop who just ticketed you, the boss, the difficult friend, or even the homeless person on the street. You know how to be respectful, so be respectful to your kids. Your kids need it from you, and it will pay off with great benefits.

The third tool to be an effective parent is *discipline:* constructive, effective discipline. By the way, discipline and punishment are two different things. The goal of discipline is to teach or train. The goal of punishment is to cause pain for wrong doing. It needs to be our goal to discipline our children in the most positive ways.

Let me first tell you what the least effective discipline strategies are: yelling, threatening, spanking, lecturing, and grounding. When I tell that to my clients, they give me this look and then ask me, "If I can't do those things, what else is there?" It is sad, but it is what most of us learn to do as parents. Anyway, as you probably know, those techniques only work short term, cause resentment, or don't work at all.

What does work? Before I give you some specifics of what does work, let me give you an effective principle to keep in mind. Your goal in parenting is not to control your child, but to motivate them to do what is best.

There are two ways to motivate a person: positive reinforcers, or negative consequences.

Positive Reinforcers	Negative Consequences
Money	Fines
Freedom	Work
Experiences	Loss of privileges
Places	Loss of possessions
Privileges	Time outs

To best discipline you child, you'll need to use a combination of both positive reinforcers and negative consequences. It's always better to go positive if possible. Kids will more likely alter behavior if it gets them more of what they want, which is usually money or freedom as positive experiences. Of course, we all respond better to affirmations and positive attention.

However, there will be times that you'll need to assign work (community service) as a consequence. Kids can pull weeds, pick up trash, wash dishes, and clean floors. Some may be more motivated by the fear of being fined, or having to write an essay, or losing their computer and phone privileges. Make consequences short term and deliver with respect, not anger. If you train up a child correctly, it is likely they will stay on the path of success. If parents can be unified and create an environment of healthy love and appropriate discipline, then "the kid's touch" will bring about a much better marriage.

Chapter 7

The Financial Touch

Research reveals that financial issues are one of the biggest reasons for marital discord and conflict. We have the tendency to fight about money. Couples are stressed because of the level of debt that many are facing. However, couples with plenty of money have as much conflict about the subject as those experiencing financial struggles. It's a sensitive subject for most people, and leads to many problems in their marriages.

To create the happy marriage that you both desire, you are going to need a plan to overcome the problem. So what exactly is the problem? Why does money trigger so much emotion and potential conflict? It has to do with fear. Fear is the real problem. We are scared that we can't pay our bills, scared that we will lose out nest egg. We're scared that we will need money for an emergency, scared that we won't have enough for retirement. We are scared about money. We often base our security upon our financial portfolio. We all need a sense of security, stability, and safety. People have strong reactions when their security is threatened, and that reaction is usually anger. Expressing anger will almost always lead to conflict, hence the problem with money.

Well, if fear is the problem, what is the solution? First I'll tell you what is not the solution. More money won't fix the problem. Better budgeting and financial planning won't necessarily fix the problem. Remember, the problem is fear and how you communicate your fear. This chapter is not about fixing your financial problems. It is about fixing how you deal with your financial problem and how it adversely affects your marriage. You can actually fix you financial problem and yet continue to have conflict about money. I see it all the time.

The solution must be about dealing with fear and communication. Fear is simply a signal that triggers certain brain chemistry which causes an emotional and physical reaction within a person. From that point on, everyone decides how to proceed and react to that signal. It's like when your oil or engine light comes in on your car. It is a signal letting you know there is a potential problem. Some people react quickly and strongly to an engine light, others may ignore the light for months. It is the same with the fear signal. Fear lets you know there is a potential problem. You may be in danger. You then decide how to deal with that fear. When it comes to money, many people get into a control mode or an anger mode. Being in control or feeling anger helps reduce the feeling of fear. Unfortunately, moving from fear to anger or control will often cause relationship problems.

My suggestion is to do something else with your fear. Here are some ideas:

- Talk calmly about your anxiety and fears. Discuss ways to alleviate your fears. Develop some ideas and plan together.
- Utilize your faith and spirituality to give you comfort. Pray, read scripture, memorize verses pertaining to fear and anxiety. There are more verses about this subject than any other subject in the Bible. God knew we would struggle with anxiety.
- Develop an attitude of thankfulness. Being thankful will help reduce fear. It says in Philippians 4:6-7: *"Do not be anxious about anything, but in everything, by prayer and petition, with thanksgiving, present your requests to God, and the peace of God, which transcends*

all understanding, will guard your hearts and minds in Christ Jesus." As you develop your faith with a thankful heart, you'll find fear becoming less of a problem.

- Some people are genetically predisposed to anxiety. Their brains are wired chemically to cause a person to struggle with fear. Medication can be helpful if your anxiety and fear are too much to manage on your own. It doesn't mean that you are weak or not spiritual enough. It means you have a biological problem that you can't fix without medical intervention.

Poor communication skills are the other main factor that contributes to problems with money. Keep in mind that your conflict over money is not because of the money. It is because of how you communicate about money. When communication about money breaks down, then you end up disagreeing about how to handle finances. Obviously, going in different directions with the money leads to more conflict and anger. Consider the following suggestions:

- Don't discuss money when you are angry. If you start getting angry, take a time out and cool down.
- Express your fears and concerns. Your partner will be more receptive to hearing about your fears than about your anger.
- Decide to work together as a team to manage your money. Don't work independently or try to control everything.
- Be open and honest about your financial situation. Your spending and debt can't be kept a secret.
- Have a business meeting. Start with identifying the problem. Write the problem at the top of a piece of paper. Then have a brainstorming session. Write down any ideas about fixing the problem. Don't criticize any of the brainstorming

ideas. Just write down each idea. Then go over each idea one at a time. Both of you have equal power to veto any suggestion. If an idea is vetoed, scratch it off the list. No need to argue about it or defend it. Just go to the next idea. After you are done, you may have a possible solution to implement. If for some reason all the ideas are vetoed, then start over with the process and try to come up with new solutions. If that doesn't work, consider the help of a mediator or counselor.

- Develop a plan of implementation utilizing the possible solutions. Decide who is going to do what and when.

Hopefully, if you are able to use some of these suggestions, you'll find yourselves attacking the problem instead of each other. Your communication skills will work for you instead of against you. It is possible to work together even in the light of financial troubles. Having the right financial touch will strengthen your marriage and bring about more satisfaction in your relationship.

Chapter 8

The Emotional Touch

Being able to connect on both physical and emotional levels is the core to real and deep intimacy. That intimacy brings about a lasting and satisfying marriage.

The emotional touch is generally more significant to women, whereas most men are focused on the physical touch. However, men also need emotional intimacy just as women want and need physical intimacy.

It is crucial to understand that for most women to desire and respond to physical intimacy, they must first have the emotional intimacy. Without emotional intimacy, it is difficult for women to open the door of their sexuality. Men are quite the opposite and are easily turned on physically. For men, being sexually intimate actually opens the door to being more emotionally intimate.

So, you can see this leads to a bit of a problem. Women need emotional connection before sexual intimacy, while men are more able to connect emotionally after sexual intimacy.

Well, I have bad news for you guys. The only way it's going to work well is if you first meet the emotional intimacy needs of your spouse before you get your sexual needs met. There's no sense in arguing or pouting about it either. It's just the way it is. Women are designed that way and it can't be changed. So if you want your sexual needs met, focus first on attending to her emotional needs.

Now that I have hopefully convinced you, let's

take a look at the emotional touch and how best to accomplish this. In order to get the right touch, you will need to understand the emotional language of your spouse. If you can figure out the emotionally connecting language for your spouse, then you will be more successful in connecting with the emotional touch.

For men, the emotional touch can be words of encouragement and appreciation, spending time with them, doing fun things together, and of course, the physical touch. When you do these things for men, it helps them to feel close and connected. As a result, men will feel more inclined to attend to their spouse.

Women, however, tend to need a deeper level of connection that involves emotional sharing. Quit rolling your eyes, guys. Women need to know how you feel. They want you to get in touch with who you are, what you think, what you're feeling, and then to share it with them. That requires something most men are not familiar or comfortable with. Men grow up trying to suppress and control their emotions, not identifying them or sharing them with others.

Here are some suggestions to get you started. First, set aside time to focus on your spouse without interruption from outside sources. Second, sit face to face so you are able to maintain eye contact. Third, start sharing your thoughts and feelings. Talk about you goals, your passion, your fears, your ideas, your past, your future, and your relationship. Share anything you want, especially about how you feel.

Keep a few things in mind here. Guys typically don't know how to do this, nor do they want to do this. So we need a little help getting started. Guys, you need to be willing and available to make this happen. You'll find that it's not so bad. You'll be meeting the emotional needs of your spouse, who in turn will most likely meet your sexual needs. So ladies, be patient, positive, and constructive in this process or you will discourage this from happening. Ask questions to get things started. Be a good listener, not giving instruction or criticism. There are a lot of feelings inside men, and with a little positive encouragement they will eventually open up. Guys, you also need to listen, show empathy, and be positive without trying to solve or cut short the problem.

By doing this together, you're likely to increase emotional connection and intimacy which will obviously improve your marriage. There are also other ways to meet the emotional needs of your spouse. Again, it depends on their emotional language. It would be a good idea to sit down and discuss with each other the things that would help you feel emotionally intimate.

It may be non-sexual intimacy which we'll cover in the next chapter. It may be love notes and letters. Or it may be spending time doing something together, something that makes you feel close. It might be picking flowers, dancing, or having a candlelit dinner. The list can go on indefinitely. The key is to specifically figure out what your spouse needs in order to feel that emotional connection and intimacy that will lead to more fulfilled physical intimacy. The emotional touch is the foundation to truly having an intimacy that creates the bond to a fulfilling marriage.

Chapter 9

The Affectionate Touch

Touch is critical to life, especially to the life of a relationship. Maybe you've heard the story about the children found in Romania's notorious orphanages at the fall of communism. Children were discovered strapped to beds in state hospitals, undersized, underfed, and under loved. Their condition, known as failure to thrive, was directly linked to almost complete absence of affection, positive touch, or human interaction. It was also discovered that some of the babies who were doing better had received more touching and caring from nurses that took the time to pick up and hold these children.

Researchers have found that the absence of touch can lead to brain damage. Monkeys kept in isolation at the University of Illinois suffered brain damage, while those living in unhampered natural colony remained unaffected.

Massage therapists commonly experience tears on their massage beds as women, who have not been touched by their husbands for years, break down when they feel the therapist's hands on their skin. These women will spend hundreds of dollars each year on massage, just to be touched.

As you can see, these studies reflect our need for human touch. It is especially critical to developing intimacy and connection in your marriage. I want to differentiate here between affectionate touch and sexual touch. The affectionate touch I am referring to is nonsexual. Sometimes nonsexual touch can lead to or even feel sexual. But the point here is to learn how to give affectionate touches without it being sexual or having the goal of leading to sex.

Both men and women need affectionate touch. In general, though, men tend to more quickly desire sexual touch and can leave out an adequate amount of nonsexual touching. The difference is that men feel more loved and connected with sexual touch. Women feel more loved and connected with nonsexual touch. You see, women want to know that you want and desire them apart from their bodies. If they know that, then they will feel loved for who they are, not just because they have the right body parts. If a woman only gets love and affection when a man wants her sexually, she will eventually get resentful and begin withholding her body until she feels loved as a person. This may not be a conscious decision on her part. A woman whose husband is non-sexually affectionate with her opens up and wants to share herself with him. A woman whose husband is giving her mostly sexual touches draws away from him because it feels damaging to be wanted only for sex. She may feel she is being taken advantage of or used.

What often happens is that women begin to fear that affectionate touching will always lead to sex. As a result, they may stop giving affectionate touches to their husband and withdraw from their husband's affectionate touches. This is why it is so important to provide affectionate touches without sexual intentions. Women especially need to feel loved, and enjoy touch apart from it becoming sexual.

The following list will give you some ideas on effective affectionate touching:

A. Sit close together when watching TV and use the time for physical touch.

B. Pay attention to how much physical contact you have on a daily basis. Touch often and maintain lots of eye contact. Kiss regularly, with lots of hugs.

C. Spend a lot of time holding hands. Think of different ways to enjoy touching each other's hands, and the feelings it conveys.

D. Begin each day with a few minutes of cuddling and nonsexual touching before getting out of bed. This is a good time to speak words of love and affirmation that will help you feel connected.

E. End each day with some cuddling and snuggling along with some special words, before you go to bed. Establish the habit of maintaining some physical contact while you are going to sleep.

F. Try to go to bed at the same time your partner does.

G. Caress your spouse's face or softly touch their body in nonsexual areas.

H. Take time giving each other massages. Communicate what feels good, and what you would like your partner to do. Try massaging each other's feet or hands using lotion or oil to enhance the feelings of touch when you massage.

I. Spend time kissing and holding each other. Show your partner the kiss you really like. Work on developing new ways to kiss.

J. Set aside time to practice giving each other nonsexual

touches. Set a date and focus on pleasuring each other in nonsexual ways.

K. As you work on adding more affectionate touches, keep the lines of communication open so you can learn what does or does not work. The affectionate touch requires not only a nonsexual touch, but also a soft touch. A woman's skin is about ten times more sensitive than a man's.

These are just a few ways to increase the affectionate touch in your relationship. There are a multitude of other affectionate touches. Talk about it. Be creative and do it. The affectionate touch will be helpful in increasing emotional intimacy, and will also help you achieve more positive sexual intimacy. Let's move on to chapter ten to figure out some ways to improve our sexual touch.

Chapter 10

The Sexual Touch

Is this it? The climax of this book? Is this the pinnacle of the hard work we have discussed this far? Many would say "yes, yes, yes, we finally got here." Others would say "I knew he would get here, this was written by a man."

Regardless of your views on sexuality, the reality is that it is a big deal. It sometimes seems our world revolves around sex. So it needs to be addressed. It's very important, whether you want it to be or not. On the other hand, for too many, sex is way too important, and it is the only goal.

Our libido (sex drive) is part of who we are. It is not easy to find a way to be a healthy, sexual, functioning person. Too many of us are out of control or too many don't have the freedom or joy of being sexual. The sexual touch is the most powerful touch in an intimate relationship. It has so much power to destroy, as well as the power to help bring a couple to the ecstasy of intimacy.

Sex is very much like fire. It can bring warmth, light, and purpose. But it can also hurt and cause severe damage. I want to help you know how to build a fire and how to use the fire to achieve your intended purpose.

Being an avid camper, I know a little about building fires. There are basically three ways to build a fire. The first is you take your time putting together the necessary ingredients such as paper, kindling, small branches, large pieces of wood, and matches. That kind of fire will start slowly, get bigger, and burn longer. It works best to cook and get warm with the least work to maintain in the long run. It does take more work initially. However, once it's burning it only needs replenishing ingredients to keep it going.

The second kind of fire is built using some paper, a store bought fake log, and then you add some wood. This type of fire is much easier to get started. There is a lot less work involved in the beginning. There are two problems with this kind of fire. The first problem is that because the fire didn't gradually build and get hot enough, the logs will not catch fire, and when the log burns out, the fire goes out. The second problem is that it is dangerous to cook over the fake logs because of the ingredients used to make this type of fire.

The third kind of fire is the one teenagers usually build. They get some wood together in a big pile, pour gas or lighter fluid on it, and then light it. All at once you have a big fire. Unfortunately, it is very dangerous.

Okay, so what does all this have to do with sex? Let me explain. The last type of fire building I described is usually made by those who know the least about fire building, and do the most damage. It's the same in the sexual arena. These people often cause great damage trying to make sex happen without using the right ingredients, and by trying to do too much too fast. It ends up blowing up in their face. The following are examples of those who operate in this fashion:

A.   Anyone who forces sex or any kind of sexual experience without the consent of their partner. This includes if your partner is asleep or passed out for any reason. Sex without a willing partner is extremely damaging. Needless to say, this includes anyone who is under age. Being married doesn't give you the right to your spouse's body unless it's okay with them.

B.   People who rush into sex without commitment, love, and a relationship that has been built over time, are setting themselves up to be burned by the power of sex. These people are setting themselves up for unwanted pregnancies, S.T.D.'s, emotional pain, and significant grief.

C.   Individuals that use wrong ingredients such as swingers, prostitution, and infidelity. It may be exciting at the time, but I guarantee it won't work over time and you'll be damaged.

The second type of fire, the one created by artificial ingredients, is like those individuals that use pornography. The fire certainly starts easily. But like a fire with a fake log, it doesn't create the long lasting intimate love that we truly desire.

Obviously, men are turned on by pornography. However, because it is not real, it leads to unrealistic expectations. This results in men needing more and more stimulation to achieve fulfillment. In addition, most women are offended by it, and it will lead to relationship problems. You may have an easy fire, but it won't last. Plus it will be dangerous to yourself and your relationship. This kind of behavior tends to pull you in and create a prison that is hard to escape. It pulls you further and further in, all the while making you less and less content.

Pornography for women can be found in romance novels and movies. Women can get addicted to the feelings that these types of entertainment provide. They then think that the average guy is supposed to act like what they read about or see in the movies. This leads to disappointment and unrealistic expectations, causing conflict and hurt.

In order to have a healthy sexual relationship with your partner, it requires the right ingredients at the right time. Here's what it looks like:

- Women, like a good fire, need time and the right kind of touches to respond sexually. In fact, foreplay starts well before any kind of sexual touching. To light their fire, most women need to feel loved, romanced, and connected with their spouse. It's why this is the last chapter. The stage for sex is set by operating well in the nine previous touches.

- Men don't need the same when it comes to sex. In fact, for men, the sexual touch should be chapter one, not chapter ten. However, the reality is that if you want a good, lasting fire, it will have to be built gradually and with the right ingredients.

- Romance is the spark that gets the fire going once all the ingredients are in place. Romance does not mean being directly sexual. Romance can be a kiss, loving words, a special look, a candlelight dinner, dancing, cuddling, or a host of other loving behaviors. Check with your partner to see what is romantic to her.

- Once the fire is lit, proceed slowly. Let the flame build. The main complaint of most women is that men move way too fast. Be slow. Touch her body softly in the nonsexual areas before proceeding to the sexual zones. Remember, she needs to build up to being touched sexually. In fact, if you touch a woman's nipples or vagina too soon, it may turn her off, not on.

- If you're not familiar with a woman's body and her sexually sensitive areas, then read a few sex books and educate yourself. A woman's clitoris is where the action is. If you want to satisfy your partner, learn where it is and how to touch it. A man's body is pretty easy. Just touch anywhere and we are ready to go.

- Be willing to talk to your partner before, during, and after sex. It is connecting as well as educational when you can communicate about what works and about what doesn't.

- Be willing to do sexual touches that please your partner. This may include kissing all over, body massages, caressing her hands during lovemaking, cuddling before and after, touching her hair, oral sex, soft teasing touches that build, undressing slowly, or dressing sexually. Talk about the sexual touches that turn you on so that you both know what the other really likes.

- Maintain your emotional connection during sex with eye contact, words of love, and being responsive and attentive to what your spouse may be needing or enjoying.

- Don't be too rough, too fast, too smelly, too pushy, too focused on your own needs or performance, too distracted (turn off the T.V.), too distant, too cold, or too unresponsive.

Hopefully, these suggestions about the sexual touch will improve your sex life. This short chapter obviously can't begin to cover everything couples need to learn to maximize their sex life. I would recommend that you read a few good books on the subject, such as John Gray's book, *Mars and Venus in the Bedroom.*

The sexual touch will work best if you are applying the other nine touches. To make your relationship what you both want it to be, make a commitment to each other that you will do your best to implement these ten touches. It will change your marriage.

Chapter 11

The Spiritual Touch

You may be wondering why I'm including a chapter about spirituality, and how that directly affects your marriage. To begin, if you're a believer, then you probably know two things. One, it was God who set up the whole idea of marriage in the first place, so he must have some thoughts about what will make it work. Two, God is love and what most marriages need is more love.

The purpose of this chapter is to help you apply healthy spiritual principles to your marriage, so that it will actually help your marriage work well. I have heard too many stories about people applying unhealthy spirituality to their marriage, and it causing major damage. What is healthy spirituality, and how can that make my marriage better?

Let's start by trying to get a glimpse or maybe even a picture of what that looks like. Of course the picture I will be creating for you comes out of my own spirituality. I am sure I don't know or have all the truth, so I suggest that whatever I say you need to check it out with God, with scripture, and with other Christians. I base my position on the foundation of true Christianity. Unfortunately, much of Christianity has turned into another false religion with a lot of do's and don'ts. I have written another book titled "Why Christianity Isn't Working" that explores many of the false ideas of the "Christian" religion. True Christianity does work.

My goal in this brief chapter is to touch on the basic principle of true Christianity and how that can impact your marriage in a positive way.

I had a client, I'll call John, in my office a couple of weeks ago who shared with me the turning point in his life happened seven years ago when he had a near death experience after an auto accident. John said he temporarily died and had an encounter with God who said he wasn't finished here and that He had something more for him to do. I asked John what was the most significant thing he gained from that experience. John replied quickly with, "God is real."

I have got news for you...God is real. Believe what you want, it doesn't change the facts. Reality is what matters and we will all see one day that God is real. Given that reality, we must make a decision that starts with believing or choosing not to. Either takes faith since we don't know in a tangible or physical sense. I have met people and even have friends that don't believe God exists because of the pain and evil in this world that they have seen or encountered. They chose not to believe, which takes as much faith, maybe more, than to believe. It's true we live on a planet that is full of evil and pain. Life is hard and it does appear at times there must not be a God. Regardless, God is real and I hope you have chosen to believe.

So let's say you do believe. Wonderful, but now you have another decision. Do you want this God to be involved in your life; do you want His help, His direction, and His comfort? If so, are you willing to pursue Him, seek after Him, get to know Him, and even obey Him? It's a nice thing to believe in God, but it doesn't do a lot of good unless you have some kind of relationship with Him.

Much of the problem with wanting to pursue God, and have Him be directly involved in your life is an inability to actually trust Him, believing that He really is good and has your best interest in mind. Life has taught us something very different. Life has taught us not to trust, bad things happen, we will suffer emotionally and physically. Life can really suck, excuse my French, it's just the best word for the reality that we experience.

Now if God is really there and is really good, why would He allow life to be so difficult and painful? Am I really supposed to believe He loves me and I can trust Him? As a result we don't really pursue Him, we only trust Him when life is good. We are not convinced that it even does much good. In addition to all that, we are not really sure how to do it anyway, so we either don't try much or we focus too much on being "good".

What I have discovered about human nature is that we are inclined to do the easy thing. We don't naturally want to grow or mature. We don't want the pain and difficulty of life. Why God does it have to be so hard? Why? Because we are less inclined to depend on God or to grow and learn without pain. Pain is necessary for growth. If you look back in your life it is likely that you grew most and sought God most when you were in pain. God is good and loves you beyond what we could imagine, however He wants us to grow up spiritually and emotionally. He wants us to become like Him. Unfortunately, we probably need some pain to accomplish that.

So what has this got to do with marriage? One of the main things we are here to learn is how to love better. What better environment to learn how to love than marriage. Being with the opposite sex all the time can be so different and sometimes so difficult. God wants us to love better and better. We can learn and practice daily with our spouse. Sometimes it is painful and difficult, but nonetheless it is what we are here for, to love.

A healthy relationship with God is critical to developing the desire and ability to love not only our spouse but others, even our enemies. A healthy relationship with God is based on recognizing who God is and who we are from his perspective.

God is good. He is holy and created a perfect universe with perfect people. His one mistake, if you want to call it that, was to give humans free will. Without free will there can be no genuine love. But free will allowed evil to enter the perfect place He created and it's been going downhill ever since, but God wanted love so he has allowed it. Unfortunately, our choices separated us from God but his love caused Him to provide a way to make us holy like Him so we could be in relationship with Him, now and forevermore. That provision is His son Jesus Christ who came for the purpose of sacrificing himself so the price for our sin would be paid. The price was death. As a result, we only need to believe and choose to have Jesus to be our Lord and Savior. We then will receive His Spirit which is holy-the Holy Spirit and now our sins are not counted against us and we become the righteousness of Christ according to scripture. We are now new creations who God adopts into His family.

God's love is not dependent on us or how good we are. Our relationship is now based on faith, the more we realize how unconditional His love is (read about the prodigal son) and how completely forgiven we are-even though we continue to sin, we will grow to love Him more and more, allowing His Spirit to work in us which will bear the fruit of love.

When our relationship is bases on how well we are obeying God then we will either live in condemnation and guilt or in self-righteousness because we think we are being good enough. It's not about us and what we do. It's about Him and what He's done for us.

Our part is to believe, accept and recognize the truth of Him and who we are to Him. A healthy spirituality is freedom to be who we are and know we are loved and accepted. When we fail, we recognize His forgiveness and the price that has been paid.
As we pursue God and know Him more intimately then obedience and love flow out of that. We don't have to work so hard at obeying-it flows out of love, not out of obligation and fear. As we grow in love then obviously our spouse will benefit from that and our marriage will improve.

Ephesians says "The only thing that counts is faith expressing itself through love." Loving your spouse in the ways he/she needs to be loved is the answer to creating a healthy, happy marriage. It is only through God and His Spirit that we can adequately do that. As you have already experienced loving your spouse can be one of the most difficult things on earth to do. In order to accomplish your goal allow Him to help you, allow Him to live through you as you pursue Him and learn to love Him.

Love Touch Exercise

To start making changes quickly in your marriage I have devised the Love-Touch Exercise. If you will take 30 minutes a day for the next 30 days to do this, then you will immediately see positive changes in your marriage. Even after the 30 days I would recommend you continue to do this on a regular basis. Determine what will work best for you and your spouse. But in the beginning, to get the ball rolling in a positive direction, I recommend this exercise every day.

First, determine the best time each day to set aside 30 minutes to focus on each other. Put it on the calendar. Don't let anything take precedence over this time.

Second, the goal of this time is to connect with each other in a positive, non-sexual manner without external distractions. This includes T.V., movies, computer, kids, other people, phone calls, or anything else that might interfere with the two of you focusing on each other.

Third, determine what will be most effective during this time. Sit down together and make a list.

Here are some ideas:

- Give non-sexual massages

- Play cards or a board game

- Read a book together aloud

- Go for a walk

- Learn how to touch or kiss each other in more pleasing ways

- Go to the park

- Have an indoor or outdoor picnic

- Practice dancing together

- Spend time connecting spiritually with prayer or a Bible study

- Snuggle together on the couch

- Sit in front of a fireplace

- Lay in a hammock

Fourth, this is not a time to discuss problems or bring up negative issues. Keep it positive, keep it pleasant, and make it fun. If you have some different issues that need to be addressed, then do it at another time, not during your love-touch time.

Fifth, feel free to extend the time if you both desire. Also feel free to move it into the sexual arena, after the 30 minutes, if you're so in inclined. Remember though, the goal is not sex, and the Love-Touch Exercise is to be non-sexual, connecting time.

Sixth, continue to communicate to each other about how this time is working, and what you can do to keep making it better.

Seventh, keep in mind that this exercise alone without implementing the other 11 love touches will not be as effective. Keep on track with working out all 11 love touches to create the marriage that works for both you and your spouse.

Made in the USA
San Bernardino, CA
25 March 2014